Secrets OF THE Garden

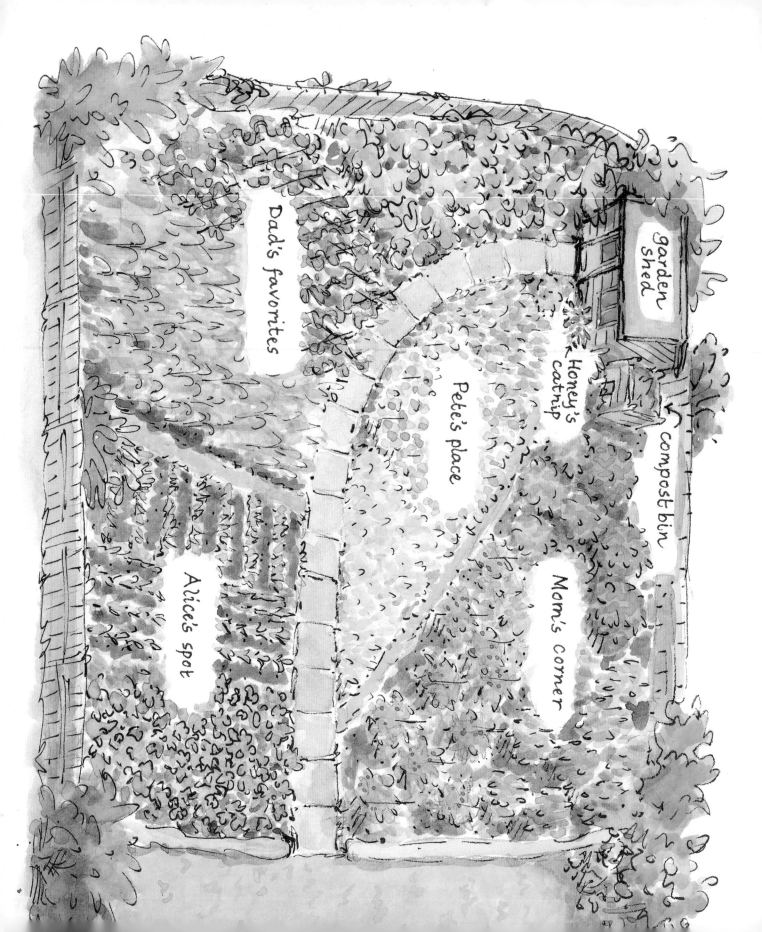

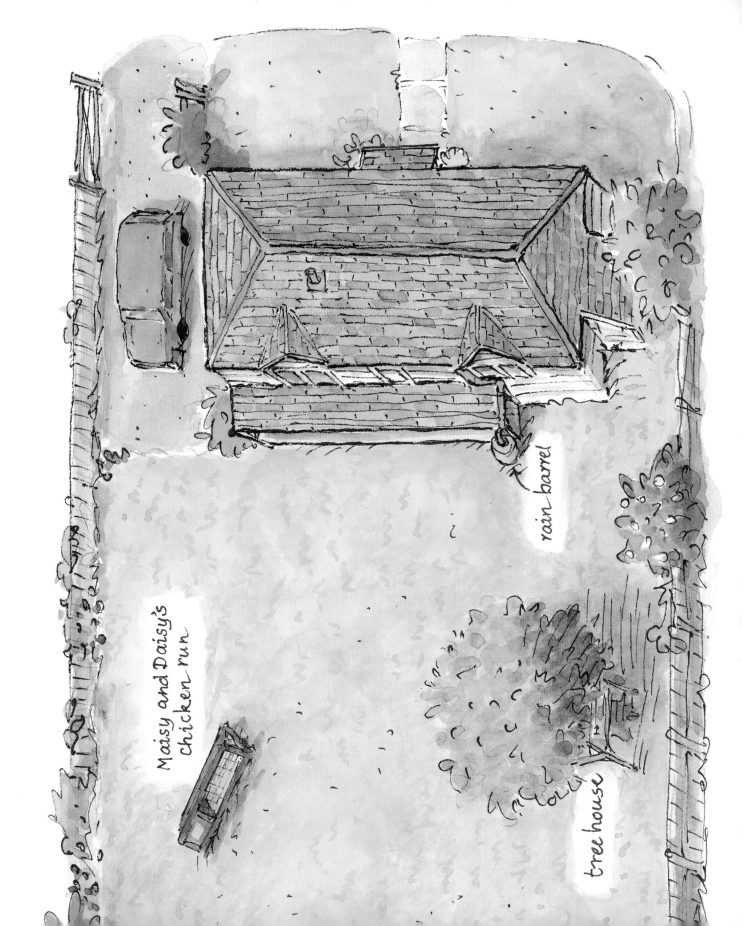

rain barrel

Maisy and Daisy's chicken run

tree house

For my mom, Beatrice Coletti Weidner,
who could grow the best tomatoes I've ever tasted –K.W.Z.

To my mother-in-law, Mary Hayward,
for whom all plants flourish –P.L.

Visit us on the Web! randomhouse.com/kids

Educators and librarians, for a variety of teaching tools, visit us at RHTeachersLibrarians.com

The Library of Congress has cataloged the hardcover edition of this work as follows:
Zoehfeld, Kathleen Weidner.
Secrets of the garden : food chains and the food web in our backyard / Kathleen Weidner Zoehfeld ; illustrated by Priscilla Lamont.
p. cm.
Summary: Depicts a family of four who make their garden their summer home as they prepare
the soil, plant seeds, water the garden, and watch for a harvest of vegetables.
ISBN 978-0-517-70990-0 (trade) — ISBN 978-0-517-70991-7 (lib. bdg.) — ISBN 978-0-375-98730-4 (ebook)
[1. Gardens—Fiction. 2. Gardening—Fiction. 3. Food chains (Ecology)—Fiction.] I. Lamont, Priscilla, ill. II. Title.
PZ7.Z715Se 2012 [Fic]—dc23 201103059

ISBN 978-0-385-75364-7 (pbk.)

MANUFACTURED IN CHINA
10 9 8 7 6 5 4 3 2 1

First Dragonfly Books Edition

Food Chains and the
Food Web in Our Backyard

Secrets
OF THE
Garden

by
KATHLEEN WEIDNER ZOEHFELD

illustrated by
PRISCILLA LAMONT

Dragonfly Books ⟶ New York

It's spring, and the days are getting longer. The sunshine warms the earth. It's time to plant the garden!

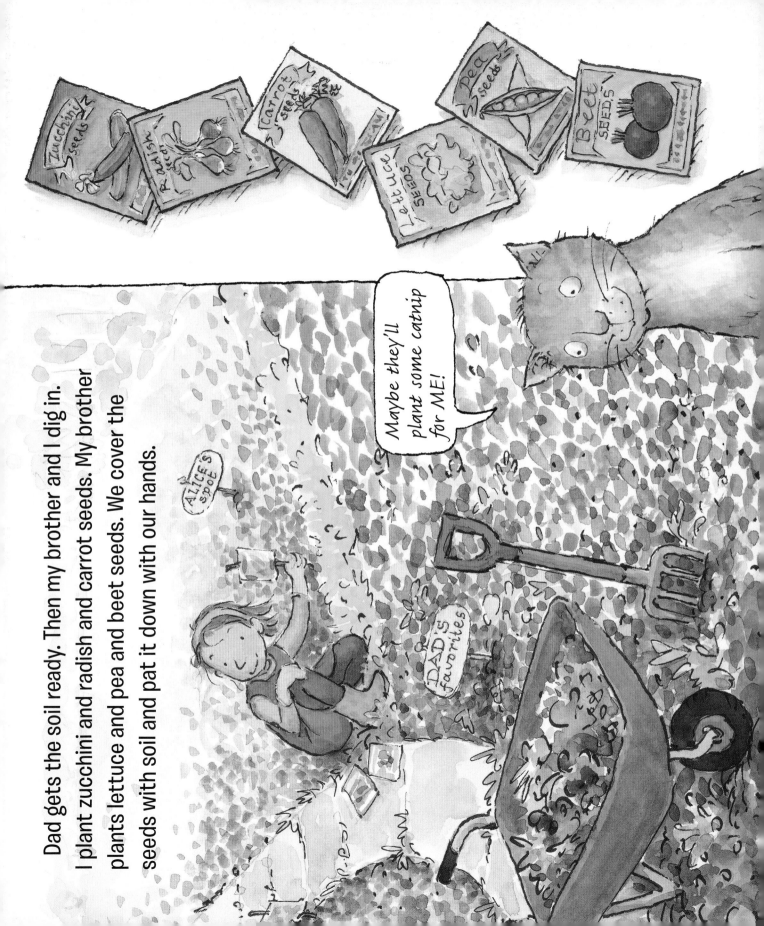

Dad gets the soil ready. Then my brother and I dig in. I plant zucchini and radish and carrot seeds. My brother plants lettuce and pea and beet seeds. We cover the seeds with soil and pat it down with our hands.

Then we watch the sky. I'm hoping to see some rain clouds. But the sky is clear and blue! We hook up the hose, and a rainbow sparkles in its spray.

A good, long rain would help.

I don't see anything!

Patience.

Old leaves and vegetable scraps—along with a little poop from our coop—make good compost to add to the soil.

Billions of tiny bacteria digest the vegetables, leaves, and scraps. That process releases nutrients that are good for growing plants.

I try to imagine what's going on under that soil. Are our seeds alive and growing? Every morning we hurry out of bed and check to see if anything has sprouted. But days go by, and still our garden looks like an empty patch of brown.

Then one morning my brother calls out. He is the first to see. I run over and bend down close to the ground. And I see them, too. Tiny sprouts are poking up through the soil.

Here are some different sprouting plants:

beet

zucchini

spinach

potato

tomato

Sprouts send roots down into the soil. They push their tiny stems up above the soil. Soon two little leaves unfold on each stem. Then more leaves grow.

Each day our sprouts grow a little bigger. Soon they are big enough to be called seedlings.

Early in spring, Mom planted tomato and green pepper seeds in small pots. She kept them warm indoors by a sunny window. Now her seedlings are ready to go in the garden. She puts potatoes the size of marbles in the ground, too. They will sprout more quickly than potato seeds.

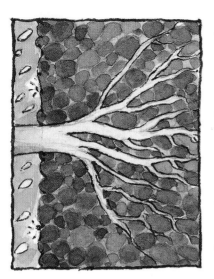

A plant's roots take in water and nutrients from the soil.

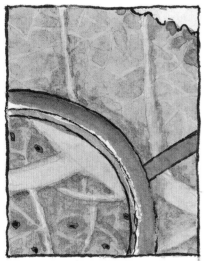

Tiny holes on the underside of each leaf take in air.

The green leaves of a plant catch sunlight.

Sunshine, fresh air, water, and soil help the seedlings in our garden grow.

Our lettuce and radishes are the first plants ready to eat. We nibble the sweet green leaves and crunch the spicy red roots.

But something, or someone, is enjoying the vegetables as much as we are.

I look for a good place to hide, tiptoe in, and sit very still. You wouldn't believe the things I see! Our little garden is filled with life

Many types of animals eat plants. People eat plants, too. Plants are the first link in any food chain. There are many different, interconnected food chains in the garden.

a short food chain

lettuce grows

rabbit eats lettuce

I spot a small brown rabbit munching lettuce. So, he's the one!
The rabbit's ear twitches, and our cat, Honey, sees it. But the
rabbit is too fast. He shoots out of the garden like a rocket.
Honey will be good at keeping the rabbit away from our lettuce.

One morning I notice some ears of corn on the ground. A few of the kernels have been nibbled. Maybe a mouse discovered the fallen ears and stopped for a snack.

Last fall Mom found an empty mouse nest on the ground under her old tomato plants. The mice had woven grass and dead leaves to make a comfortable pocket and lined it with lint and downy feathers. I wonder where the mice might be living this year.

I lie back and watch the clouds. High above, a hawk flies over. She turns back and begins to circle. Though most of the animals I see are plant-eaters, a few are meat-eaters. The hawk glides down silently. In an instant, the bird snatches a grasshopper in her claws and swoops away. Yikes! Better stay in your nest, mice!

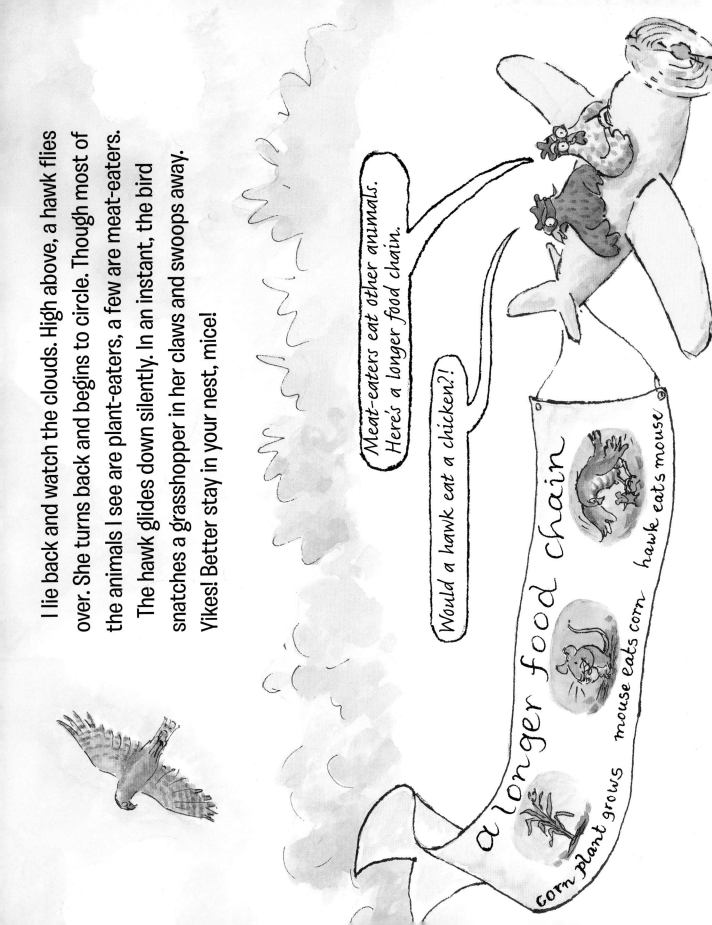

Meat-eaters eat other animals. Here's a longer food chain.

Would a hawk eat a chicken?!

a longer food chain

corn plant grows   mouse eats corn   hawk eats mouse

I like catching grasshoppers and other insects and spiders in the garden, too. But I don't eat them! Usually I watch them for a while and let them go. Once I found caterpillars gnawing on Mom's pepper plants. After that I caught as many as I could-and fed them to our chickens!

Look at this shiny bug!

It's called a potato beetle. Potato leaves are its favorite food.

Potato leaves? Yech. I don't care, as long as it doesn't eat the potato roots!

If beetles eat all the potato's leaves, the roots may die. Maybe I should dig up this plant. We could have the potatoes for supper.

Spiders are hunters. A few, like wolf spiders, stalk insects on the ground. But most, like garden spiders, build sticky webs that help them catch their prey.

another food chain

potato plant grows

beetle eats the potato leaves

spider eats beetle

a longer food chain

potato plant grows

beetle eats the potato leaves

spider eats beetle

robin eats spider

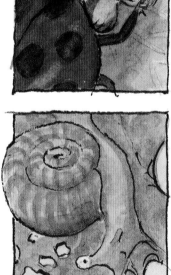

Lots of different insects are busy eating plants or other insects. The spider is busy with his beetle. They don't seem to notice that a robin has been watching. A beetle or a spider would make a good snack for a robin.

All of a sudden I see the robin scratching and pecking at the soil. He's found an earthworm. As he pulls, the worm stretches like a rubber band. Then—**snap!**—it pops out, and the bird swallows it in one gulp.

No arms, no legs, no hands, no feet. But it's a tug-of-war! Why's it so hard to pull the worm out of the ground?

He has tiny bristles that help him hang on to the walls of his burrow.

We use our cultivators to loosen up the soil around the plants so water can get down to the roots. We spread compost to add nutrients to the soil. But the worms are really better at helping the soil than we are. They work at it every day and never seem to get tired.

When plants die, they fall to the ground and begin to rot. The worms eat the rotting plants. The worms also loosen up the soil as they tunnel. Then water and air get down to the plants' roots more easily. Worms help the plants grow. The digested plant matter returns important nutrients to the soil. Worms are a special part of a food chain. As the worms tunnel around, they leave digested plant matter behind in the soil.

The plants depend on the worms and on the sunshine and fresh air.
They depend on the rain and on the good, rich nutrients in the soil.

We depend on the plants. Without them, there would be no food for animals or for people. We're all connected.

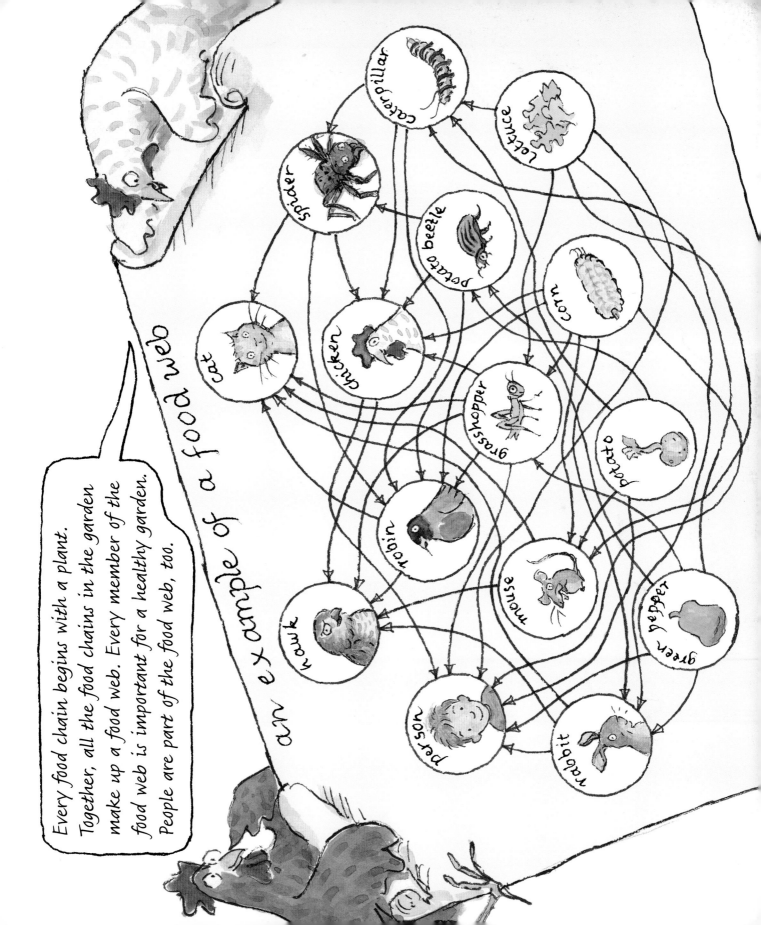

an example of a food web

Every food chain begins with a plant. Together, all the food chains in the garden make up a food web. Every member of the food web is important for a healthy garden. People are part of the food web, too.

I like to call the garden our summer home.

Our real home is made of wood. It has four walls and a roof and floor that keep out the sun and rain and dirt. It's a good house, really. But our garden home is different.

Only my family and I live in our wooden home. But in our garden home, we make way for the neighbors—for the rabbits, birds, spiders, and beetles. It is their summer home, too.

As autumn nears, the days get shorter and cooler. We harvest the vegetables that are left. The time has come to clean our tools and put them away for the winter. Time for the garden to rest.

The animals have eaten and stored fat for the winter months ahead. We are also busy storing food. We can tomatoes, pickle beans, freeze corn, and hang baskets of potatoes in the cellar.

It's a little sad saying goodbye. But I know that as we sit together through the long winter evenings, we'll be having fun planning our next garden and dreaming about the warm days of spring.

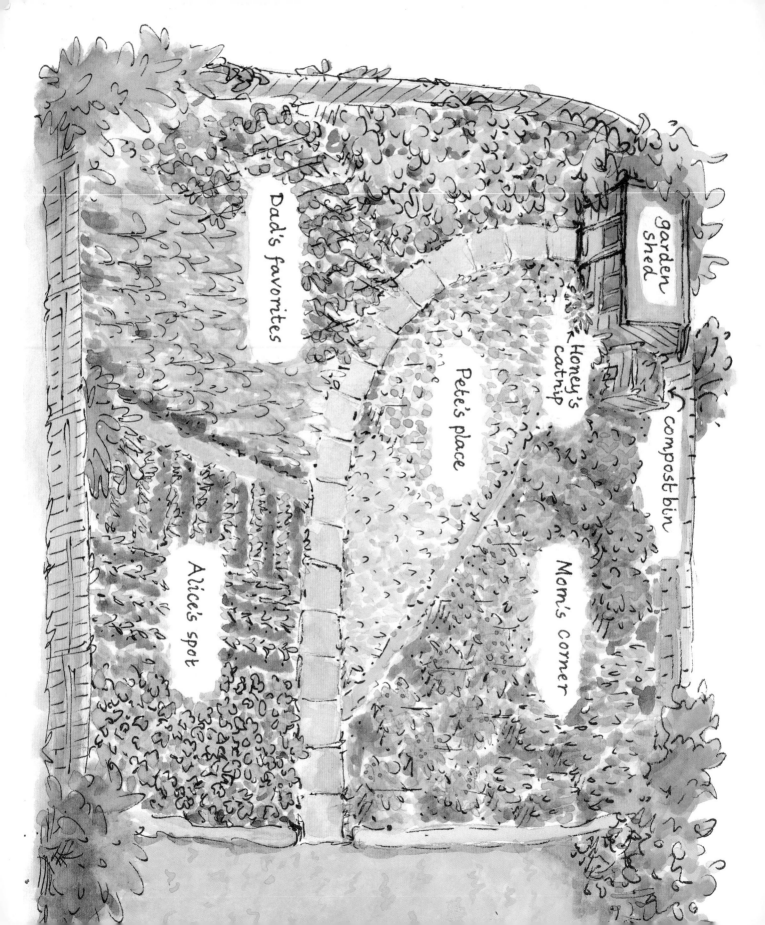

rain barrel

Maisy and Daisy's chicken run

tree house